I Can

Also by Pamela Sackett

*Two Minutes To Shine: Thirty Potent New
    Monologues for the Auditioning Actor*
Two Minutes To Shine: Book II
Two Minutes To Shine: Book III
*Two Minutes To Shine, Book IV:
    Contemporary Monologues for Mixed Ages*
Two Minutes To Shine: Book V
    (Samuel French, Inc. New York)

Speak of the Ghost: In the Name of Emotion Literacy
Saving the World Solo
Booing Death: with Shpilkes & Rhyme
*NEED FEEL WRITE: Storied Picture Prompts
    for the Brave Journaler*
    (Emotion Literacy Advocates, Seattle)

I Can

Twelve Ways
to Witness the Heart

Pamela Sackett

Copyright © 2019 Pamela Sackett.
All rights reserved.

All content written by Pamela Sackett unless other persons are named. No part of this book may be used, reproduced or transmitted in any form or by any means whatsoever without written permission from the author, except in the case of brief quotations embodied in academic research and journals, critical articles and reviews.

For information write and visit:
Emotion Literacy Advocates
www.emolit.org
info@emolit.org
www.emolit.org/I-Can-Book-details.html

ISBN#: 978-0-929904-10-8

Development consultant: Mark Magill
Book and cover design: Daniel Sackett

Toward sustainable publishing, this book is manufactured on demand to reduce supply chain waste, greenhouse emissions and conserve valuable natural resources.

Deep Gratitude
for
Daniel Sackett
&
Mark Magill

To my father—lover of words, language and meaning, lover of theatre and music, lover of life and the heart of the matter. He tried to teach me to read maps, but I resisted and yet the metaphor got in and now I'm steadfastly mapping my whole interior. He laughed big and taught me to love the water by letting me ride through it on his trusty, playful back. He sat quietly in a dusking space and knew how to ruminate, well before meditation became a western thing. He made mistakes, he kept going. Adored and adoring, he treated people as though they were his one and only, drinking in family, friends and places, endlessly, until his end arrived at a shockingly early age. I dedicate this to you, my Hungarian daddy, with tears and wonder, in an epiphanic moment, seeing your stunning influence on the values and forms I hold near and dear, aiming ardently—like you—to share and foster.

Message from Pamela

There are many roads to *Nirvana* and this booklet has none of them. Instead, I offer a road to digging into the mechanics of the mind to encourage ways of thinking that serve as the heart's witness, champion and protector.

Language is my salvation. When I didn't have an enlightened witness for my heart, especially when it was severely injured in my developing years, I had to hide it, even from myself. To find it, I searched with words, creatively, and became intimately involved with the English language and, very specifically, how it engaged me with and disengaged me from my heart. Therein laid the groundwork for my emotion literacy invention, circa 1992, zooming in on words as portals or impediments to the labyrinthine interior.

In orchestrating emotion literacy exploration as a teaching artist, working with adult and youth prison residents, parents, artists and art patrons, public and private high school students, their teachers and professionals who influence the lives of children through social services and health education, I was struck by the common thread that emerged between otherwise disparate individuals and groups, when it came to interacting with the heart part: resistance, fear and a stark absence of favorable ways to think about the vulnerability we all inhabit.

What continues to stand out is that our human culture is prone to quick-fix, security-seeking twists and turns—no matter what the circumstances—and how fight / flight / freeze modes of operation overwhelm the mind and deter the heart's transparency.

Writing for the stage, constructing high-stress characters struggling to communicate, designing performance narrative for and about special populations, calls me to examine the mind and its machinations and how ways of thinking form a bridge or a blind spot to our most tender empathic selves.

In moments when my own defenses rise up against a threat—real or imagined—and won't allow me to get next to that innermost part or even see it, understanding the barriers in my thinking process frees me to wake up to my vulnerability and reassuringly greet it.

The *I Can* book speaks to the gravity of such a greeting, offering food for thought, guidance and encouragement for your own unique configuration of the journey within.

On behalf of fully inclusive communication and insight-directed socially ethical interactions, I present my manifesto, distilled to twelve essences in progression. You may already know the vision I profess in the *I Can* book. I offer this piece of a large puzzle as a reminder of our genuinely connected worlds.

*I could tell you I've traveled far and wide—
all the places I've been*

*I could tell you the marvels
with whom I've studied—
wisdom and wit I absorbed from them*

*I could tell you I've scaled mountains—
forwards and backwards, on my knees
multitudinous trials and tribulations*

*or, I could open my mouth and beg please—
allow me to tell you of my devotion
for reasons too many to say*

*do you aim, as I do
for a kinder world within?
may I add to your mix a dozen ways?*

Twelve Ways, *abbreviated*

1st I can consider the presence of feelings 19

2nd I can take time to notice my needs and feelings 25

3rd I can name and claim feelings for their own sake 29

4th I can understand and value feelings by identifying their source 33

5th I can pay particular attention to my spoken language and thinking process 39

6th I can perceive the relationship between unknown feelings and emotional behavior 43

7th I can discern feeling-unfriendly language and revise my approach 49

8th I can accept my full range of feelings 53

9th I can host my constituency of needs 57

10th I can appreciate my feelings and needs, see them as legitimate in and of themselves 61

11th I can re-evaluate and establish new ways of regarding vulnerability 65

12th I can courageously practice, model and grow my skills 67

First Way

I CAN CONSIDER THE PRESENCE OF FEELINGS in the context of my own interior landscape, interactions I have socially and with the natural world.

When a man is able to connect with his feelings, he is able to care more.
~Warren Farrell

What is the opposite of "considering the presence of feelings"? Ignoring feelings when they are present? Fearing them? Denying feelings? Just plain not knowing or recognizing them in the moment? Not understanding or valuing them, not knowing how to interpret them?

Recognizing feelings and comprehending their language are not automatic for anyone, even the most intelligent. The process of developing this witnessing way, "considering the presence of feelings," offers an opportunity to build a feeling vocabulary. Feelings talk through sensations in the body. We can learn to read their language and we can track how our language of thought coincides.

Feelings have company. They are not loners, though sometimes, when we have them, we feel alone. Feelings are always on the go. They have travel companions in our needs, thoughts, memories and associations, values and beliefs. Do we sidestep that constellation, move around it or move with it...do we see and understand these aspects of ourselves?

The perception of feelings is influenced by how we think, what we have learned to think. Feelings, once considered through the thinking process that has shaped our lives, can inform the relationship we have to the actual experience of a feeling.

Feelings can be fuel and our thoughts guideposts to understanding our feeling senses in the moment, steering us towards or away from experiences.

A feeling can take us to a place we cherish and it can take us to a place we don't want to remember, but the feelings themselves are a gift that accompanies us through thick and thin, a gift that distinguishes us from machines.

Feelings show up in an especially desired context and one that we find repellent; they show up regardless of the nature of a context; feelings do not discriminate. By being with our feelings, letting ourselves know them, we create a home for feelings and, essentially, a vital part of ourselves has a place to live. A well-developed relationship with our feelings affords deeper understanding of ourselves and each other—a grand exploration in progress. Circumstances and particular feelings might come and go; our **capacity to feel** is a remarkable form of protection and guidance that stays with us as we learn and grow.

Feelings are non-verbal and don't need words to exist, and words help to make their presence known. Feelings come more alive when shared.

> *Is it really possible to tell someone else what one feels?*
> ~Leo Tolstoy, *Anna Karenina*

Can you tell someone else what you feel if you haven't yet told yourself?

TELLING

There's the story you tell yourself
and the story you know
which one is true
which one is you
there are the things that you say
and the things that you do
there's the you that you think of
and the you that shows through
which part is seen
which part is waiting to be seen
which part sees who

Second Way

I CAN TAKE TIME TO NOTICE MY NEEDS AND FEELINGS, discerning between activities and notions that assist or detract from my attendance to them.

*I explained to him, however, that my nature
was such that my physical needs often got
in the way of my feelings.*
~Albert Camus, *The Stranger*

In the hierarchy of needs, in some cultures, "soft" needs—the non-physical needs—are not high-ranking. It is easier to understand the loss of a home, or health, or a relative to death, or the need for food and clothing, than the less tangible loss of hope, equilibrium, loyalty of a friend or the presence of difficult memories. Feelings relative to these kinds of situations are more likely to be swept aside or be subject to evaluative thinking based on outer appearances, misunderstood behaviors or the imposed limits of time. Feelings and soft needs can and do elude us, but that doesn't mean they go away. Unrecognized, unprocessed feelings and needs get stored, reverberating into our relationship to ourselves, our life experiences and our dealings with others.

*Most people don't even think about feelings
or think* about *how they think
about feelings
or whether or not they think favorably about feelings,
so they probably just try to control them—
but you can't have feelings
and control feelings
at the same time,
and if you can't have feelings,
I mean really have them,
you can't think favorably about them.
If you can't think favorably about them,
you can't have them.
And if you can't have them,
you'd have to control them.
If you thought favorably about them
you wouldn't try to control them…
unless you're an actor.*

*~Saving the World Solo
(page 9)*

Third Way

I CAN NAME AND CLAIM FEELINGS FOR THEIR OWN SAKE and as a safeguard against unwittingly disavowing my feelings and projecting them onto another person or situation, and to discern projections placed upon me.

The best way out is always through.
~Robert Frost

Feelings are like children; they want to be seen and heard and have their presence known. Feelings are a part of us and seek acceptance. Once we have been taught that parts of ourselves do not qualify for acceptance, that some of our feelings are acceptable and others are not, we embark on a censorship mission. Once the family and cultural rules are laid down, spoken and unspoken, we begin to separate from and then banish our unpopular feelings, sometimes before we know we are having them.

These feeling-prohibitive rules are enforced, in large part, by consensus, through dismissive body language and behavior-centric spoken expressions, on billboards and their ilk, in facets of the media, and through collected members of our very own circle. As a protection, we hide our feelings so well they become invisible even to ourselves, fracturing our relationship to them.

And that imperative to keep feelings at bay, if introduced early enough, becomes internalized, deeply ingrained, a source of personal identification and alliance, placing us in a feeling-blocked default mode. Feelings and needs then move through us like frightened little creatures, dodging, festering, dwelling outside our radar, hungering for the light of recognition, becoming unwittingly resigned to the darkness.

Even among the most functional members of our society, great resources are spent on these underground feeling caves. Not recognizing that part of ourselves sets a path to complications. Self-knowledge and ownership of both feelings and needs are endowed through awareness.

> *The true opposite of depression is neither gaiety nor absence of pain, but vitality—the freedom to experience spontaneous feelings. It is part of the kaleidoscope of life that these feelings are not only happy, beautiful, or good*

but can reflect the entire range of human experience, including envy, jealousy, rage, disgust, greed, despair, and grief. But this freedom cannot be achieved if its childhood roots are cut off. Our access to the true self is possible only when we no longer have to be afraid of the intense emotional world of early childhood. Once we have experienced and become familiar with this world, it is no longer strange and threatening.

~Alice Miller, *The Drama of the Gifted Child: The Search for the True Self*

Fourth Way

I CAN UNDERSTAND AND VALUE FEELINGS BY IDENTIFYING THEIR SOURCE, relative to my immediate "soft" (non-physical) needs, memories and associations.

The past is never dead. It's not even past.
~William Faulkner

Carrying fond memories is easy. Chances are, because they are fond, we are not inclined to bury them. Feelings that accompany fond memories are likely to be readily available and easy to relive. Those feelings do not haunt us but shower us with more pleasant feelings, ones that we find easier to express, because it's easier to find permission to express them.

Difficult memories linger, along with their accompanying feelings, feelings that may not have been fully realized, understood, accepted or pleasant. Such feelings might linger in the deep recesses of our mind. Such feelings await our recognition.

Some unprocessed, memory-based feelings might come up when we are facing new experiences, especially experiences that even just slightly resemble the older experiences, the ones of which we are not fond. As complex impressionable beings, we cannot discard those feelings like we could a displeasing photograph of ourselves.

We can forget, we can deny or rationalize, but the feelings are a part of our fabric and will wait in line for a nod, pat and hug from our conscious mind. Such recognition can do wonders to keep those feelings from haunting us. When feelings don't receive our acknowledgement, they will send up a flare when we least expect it.

Thanks to our survival brain, we tend to resist the unknown of new experiences. Thanks again to our amygdala, when we are faced with something unfamiliar we might just find ourselves filling in the blank with what we do know. What we know could include a painful memory and the feelings that go with it. Like an old-fashioned movie house, our minds project onto the screen of prospective experiences, running images and scenes from a familiar reel.

It is difficult to face a blank wall—so difficult, especially for our survival brain, that sometimes we are compelled to hang one of our old memories there. By doing that, we convey to our amygdala: "It's okay, I know this, I've been here before, it's familiar." Old feelings can overlay the prospect of new experiences and masquerade as security.

The amygdala will take what it can get and be satisfied. If we overlay an unpleasant memory, we then might just avoid the new prospect altogether, giving ourselves a reason not to face the unknown, depriving us of the chance to practice facing the unknown and form a new memory, perhaps a masterpiece!

A new experience awaits us once we make room for it. Until feelings are integrated, they tend to bombard our blank walls. Giving space, attention and acceptance to old feelings can be a ticket to something brand-new—not a guarantee for an experience that is challenge-free, but a new prospect nonetheless.

> *I am not the person I know myself to be*
> *I am stronger and more secure*
> *it's a different person that breathes*
> *inside of me*
> *her reach is longer and knows for sure*
> *that this strong brings not a burden*
> *and is waiting to be retrieved*
> *this strong can see the light of day*
> *on the path that's yet to be conceived*
>
> *I am not the person I knew myself to be*
> *I am the person I am getting to know*
> *and in the knowing*
> *I become the unknown*
> *in the unknown I am free...*
>
> *~Speak of the Ghost:*
> *In the Name of Emotion Literacy*
> *"Naked and Dressed"*
> *(page 60)*

Fifth Way

I CAN PAY PARTICULAR ATTENTION TO MY SPOKEN LANGUAGE AND THINKING PROCESS to decipher the manner by which my thoughts and expressions open or close a perceptual door to feelings and needs.

*Inside of all of us there is the need
and the desire to be heard...*
~Vicktor Alexander

Simplistically, emotion literacy means the ability to read and comprehend emotions. To be emotion literate is to be well-informed about your emotions. When it comes to emotions, it seems obvious—smiling, laughing, crying—as plain as the nose on your face. Even just plain behaviors are tied to a plethora of influences: personal feelings and thinking, past experiences and memories, values, beliefs, individual orientation to societal conventions and cultural proprieties.

Given human systems, conflicting human needs and communication challenges, there is much to wade through for comprehension and fulfillment. Learning how to understand the deeper implications of any given emotion takes determination, time and guidance...and advocacy.

> *What is true is already so. Owning up to it doesn't make it worse. Not being open about it doesn't make it go away. And because it's true, it is what is there to be interacted with. Anything untrue isn't there to be lived. People can stand what is true, for they are already enduring it.*
>
> ~Eugene T. Gendlin

Sixth Way

I CAN PERCEIVE THE RELATIONSHIP BETWEEN UNKNOWN FEELINGS AND EMOTIONAL BEHAVIOR by applying non-polarized, feeling-inquisitive thinking.

*The limits of my language means the limits
of my world.*
~Ludwig Wittgenstein

Emotions and feelings, the terms themselves, have been regarded in certain schools of thought as interchangeable. However, I distinguish emotion from feeling because I view emotion as a phenomenon akin to behavior or expression, while feeling has a non-verbal language of its own. The bridge between feeling and emotion is often circuitous. It is our near-archaeological ability to unearth what underlies, what influences and what guides our particular thoughts, relative to emotion and feeling, that affords a clear communication system between the two.

A clear communication system renders congruency between feelings (especially in the context of needs) and their expression—a congruency perhaps not enjoyed since the age of four. Has a feeling-prohibitive environment prompted us to edit ourselves behind the scenes—

inciting us to forge a behavior that acts more like a shield than a direct communication—because to disclose our feelings would pose a breach of our security?

Embedded in our ways of mediating the pathway between our feelings and emotions are qualities, cues and learned limits that can be observed. Observation of how we travel between feelings and emotions can open the door of perception towards clarity and understanding. A growing capacity for understanding and well-practiced self-advocacy skills can lead to a more cooperative, empathic world within, applied at home, work and play. What a gift to say to ourselves:

> *You have complete permission to enter my mind, probing all my thoughts, looking for whatever you need to know. There is nothing I intend to hide from you. No matter what you will find, either luminous or dark, you can rest assured that in my heart I deeply love you and I want the best for you, and...I do mean you!*
> ~Franco Santoro

The freedom to know our feelings and needs and to understand their relationship to our emotion and expression is a direct benefit of our translation and advocacy abilities, abilities reached through feeling-inquisitive ways of thinking and talking. Therein lies the essential meaning of emotion literacy and its advocacy.

Common ways of thinking and talking about feelings and needs are often not feeling-inquisitive or need-permissive and stem from different parts of our brain. Numerous ways of thinking are actually prohibitive to the feelings and needs we carry, which is the very reason translation and advocacy skills are key.

Polarized, black-and-white thinking (good/bad, right/wrong, positive/negative) might work well in evaluating behavior, but is not guaranteed to be feeling-inquisitive. Black-and-white thinking follows the imperative of the amygdala, the part of our brain that leads our communication for the benefit of our physical survival. Feeling-inquisitiveness is not the job or the capability of the amygdala but the privilege of our brain's pre-frontal cortex. These brain functions are hard-pressed to harmonize, and, with ample attendance, we can recognize the source of our communication aims.

Even the most seemingly open words and expressions can mean different things to different people. Our contextual orientations to the exact same set of words can contrast, in varying degrees, from similar to somewhat different to diametrically opposed. Our values, what we've been taught, what we've experienced, and the ways we have and hold our experiences in our own minds and hearts figure into this complex correspondence. Underscoring these intricacies is whether or not we have been given permission to know and express all manner of feelings and needs, from early on. If not, we learn to brace ourselves for defense.

According to the language of feelings, we all have our own dictionary. Though feelings in essence are universal, our filters through which we know and express feelings can be unique. Have you read your dictionary today? What words can you add to your dictionary to pave the way for a deeper, more cooperative self-understanding that fuels the most resource-efficient attendance to needs?

> ...although (we) have a common destiny, each individual also has to work out his own personal salvation for himself in fear and trembling. We can help one another to find the meaning of life no doubt. But in the last analysis, the individual person is responsible for living his own life and for "finding himself." If he persists in shifting his responsibility to somebody else, he fails to find out the meaning of his own existence. You cannot tell me who I am and I cannot tell you who you are. If you do not know your own identity, who is going to identify you?
>
> ~Thomas Merton

Seventh Way

I CAN DISCERN FEELING-UNFRIENDLY LANGUAGE AND REVISE MY APPROACH in the interest of including my feelings as a telling facet of my whole story.

The greatest enemy of clear language is insincerity.
~George Orwell

Merriam-Webster says to be insincere is to "not express or show true feelings." Many would agree that an insincere person is not trust-inspiring and that trust is the bedrock of beautiful relationships. Given this, why wouldn't we all be upholding the wholesale offering of permission to express and show feelings—permission through feeling-permissive language—so we can all enjoy the benefits of sincerity on a daily basis?

What is the nature of Orwell's enemy, and why aren't we collectively *en route* to dissuade it from its misbegotten ways?

You will get no argument from me that feeling slows you down and can be messy. Having, expressing or showing true feelings is not a cakewalk, to be sure. Is hiding true feelings a choice based on a preference for tidiness? Are cultural memes still selling us on the idea of feeling-censorship through feeling-unfriendly, good/bad, right/wrong ways of thinking?

Feeling-unfriendly language, spoken and unspoken, is ubiquitous. I am not speaking here of the kind of language that presents itself like a telephone utility-pole cable—big, black and clunky (e.g., *shut up, I hate you*)—no, though that ungraceful composition is its own puzzle to solve, it is easy enough to see. The kind of thinking and talking in this instance—the nuanced kind—is sheer stuff, nearly invisible, but quite a sticky fabric of beliefs, philosophies, fears, unrecognized and unstated needs, and feelings.

...when people say they are bold, brave and beautiful, they'll really mean they recognized the subtle, insidious ways they were taught to ignore their most tenderest of feelings, rallied their forces and championed each and every one of those feelings just exactly as a super hero

*would in gallantly freeing all, each and every one,
enslaved by hunger, war and poverty.*

*~Saving the World Solo
(page 75)*

Eighth Way

I CAN ACCEPT MY FULL RANGE OF FEELINGS, knowing that each particular feeling is of equal value, even when not my preference or socially acceptable.

What would happen if you stopped fighting, and gave yourself permission to feel?
Not just the good things but everything?

~R.J. Anderson, *Ultraviolet*

What determines good from bad, and who determines this? We inherit some of these measures, these qualifiers, and on behalf of our own need to not be cast outside the circle of acceptance, we adopt such distinctions. But where do feelings live and how can they live, given these measured perimeters that are best applied to behaviors, actions and volitional expressions?

Inside of this witnessing way is a place of permission where we can invite and welcome all of our feelings, comfortable and uncomfortable. Like flowers, our feelings vary in color and tone, are true and deeply rooted. Feelings are friends helping us bloom in the growing knowledge of ourselves and each other.

Universally part of our daily experience, feelings can send us reeling with delight and disappointment, joy and grief, and, most essentially, remind us of our vital nature—our vulnerability. When read astutely, feelings can prompt our awareness of *soft* needs.

How—in a chaotic, security-driven world—can we adopt the freedom to create feeling-inclusiveness in the interest of self-knowledge, confidence and authentic social bonds?

> *We must be able to identify all the parts in a system and allow them to speak. All the parts in a group, even those we do not like or believe to be useless, must be present and supported.*
>
> ~Arnold Mindell

Ninth Way

I CAN HOST MY CONSTITUENCY OF NEEDS and acknowledge the presence of each one, whether or not I can fulfill it.

Need doesn't care about being sensible.
~Amit Kalantri

I have often watched a parent with their child in the park, on the edge of dark, announcing: "It's time to go." Of course the child, signed on whole-heartedly with the moment, with no regard for practical considerations or pressing situations (like the sun going down or dinner to be bought and prepared), does not want to leave, does not want to believe it's time for the fun to end. And the parent has other tasks to handle or other preferences or, perhaps, has just plain taken leave of interest in being in the park any longer.

Negotiation begins and ends when one need cancels out the other; but all needs are true, regardless of our inability to simultaneously accommodate them. On the other side of an unmet need is disappointment but not necessarily agony.

When one's need is acknowledged, albeit not fulfilled or not fulfillable, and one's disappointment is seen and accepted, a world of comfort ensues—the world of mutual inclusivity.

Although crying can be a reasonable way to express disappointment at any age, for a child it may be the only way to confide disappointment to those who hold the child's fate, moment by moment, in their hands. This ninth witnessing way advises: "When the confiding begins, you, as confidant, don't have to bend but to lend your ears."

And so it goes for the needs we carry within. Some lose, some win—all seek recognition and understanding.

Harmony is a wonderful thing but not nearly as powerful as awareness.
~Arnold Mindell

Tenth Way

I CAN APPRECIATE MY FEELINGS AND NEEDS, SEE THEM AS LEGITIMATE IN AND OF THEMSELVES, and confidently regard them without comparing myself to or depreciating someone else as an avenue of self-justification.

When people say they are the best,
they'll really mean
they resisted competing with anyone ever
because they would know
that all competing was really a divisive act
cooked up by none other than
those two feuding hemispheres of the brain
who never did get along and were, nonetheless,
perpetually in search of one another.

~Saving the World Solo
(page 73)

We are social beings in an interdependent society. Our need for each other is at the center of a plethora of other kinds of individual needs and that social need influences much that we do, even for those who work in solitude. We are here to connect, even when connecting is problematic. What does it mean to be me, to be you, to be us? Do you take time to address your feelings as an essential part of your identity, answering the constant call and fragility of soft needs in a competitive world?

Whether or not we are conscious of those soft needs and feelings, we are moved by them. When our soft needs live underground, unfulfilled, we develop discouraging beliefs that dissuade us from directly addressing our soft needs. Needs persist. They nudge and seek response. If our early expressions of needs were not met with open arms and a clear mirror, we just might have learned, too well, how to dis-embrace our soft needs and turn a blind eye, all the while preemptively validating self and invalidating others or invalidating self and validating others.

The efforts and energy required to avoid our soft needs or to approach them circuitously far surpasses the energy it might ultimately take to meet them head-on, and yet we proceed with what we know best, having learned need-negation too well. The amygdala rewards our efforts to stay parked in the familiarity zone, regardless of whether or not it is in our best interest to do so.

Were we to be free to counter the inertia, take our needs in hand and learn their inner workings; were we to deem our needs legitimate, at their core, via our own permission-granting authority, we just might be free enough to co-create a truly empathic, mutually inclusive life in community, a community that can make use of our survival, mother-bear brain (amygdala) *and* our thinking, explorer brain (prefrontal cortex) in tandem!

> *I think I can. I think I can. I think I can.*
> *I know I can.*
> ~Watty Piper, *The Little Engine That Could*

Eleventh Way

I CAN RE-EVALUATE AND ESTABLISH NEW WAYS OF REGARDING VULNERABILITY as a key characteristic of the human condition, by facing and bravely welcoming my own version of this universally shared state of being.

*Vulnerability is the birthplace of innovation,
creativity and change.*
~Dr. Brene Brown

Deep within our impetus to connect, to communicate and to know ourselves and each other, there is fertile ground, a place where anything can happen. In this open place, the story of vulnerability has more to tell than its stock tale of danger. In this open place, vulnerability spells the truth of uncertainty, the unending mystery, the wellspring of all possibility...dark and light.

Vulnerability is the only authentic state. Being vulnerable means being open, for wounding, but also for pleasure. Being open to the wounds of life means also being open to the bounty and beauty. Don't mask or deny your vulnerability: it is your greatest asset...be vulnerable: quake and shake in your boots with it. The new goodness that is coming to you, in the form of people, situations, and things can only come to you when you are vulnerable, i.e. open.
~Stephen Russell

Twelfth Way

I CAN COURAGEOUSLY PRACTICE, MODEL AND GROW MY SKILLS as a contributor to and beneficiary of my community.

What is true is invisible to the eye.
It is only with the heart that one can see clearly.
~Antoine de Saint-Exupery

'Tis a great centuries-old challenge: to be yourself as an individual and as a member of a group, without one position canceling out or over-shadowing the other. What does it mean to be yourself when we are multi-faceted and in a constant state of motion? As an emotion literacy advocate, the part of the self I pay particular attention to is inherent in all aspects of who we are inside—the part that truly feels, possesses needs and expresses. Strengthening the individual from within strengthens the individual within a group. Strong, communicative individuals can create strong, understanding groups.

The more we support ourselves inside, the more we can connect with others, the more we connect with others, the larger, more inclusive and connected our worlds can become. No matter how different we are on the outside, we are the same at the core. To embrace both our uniqueness and our common threads is a high ideal won through effort.

> *When people say they won*
> *they'll really mean*
> *they unfolded another layer of life*
> *within which they discovered*
> *a missing piece of themselves*
> *and that missing piece directly corresponded*
> *to the ones closest to them*
> *and how wonderful it was to know*
> *beyond a shadow of a doubt*
> *that all life has a connective pattern*
> *that reveals itself at every turn*
> *and that everybody has their turn…*
> *at the same time.*
>
> *~Saving the World Solo*
> *(page 72)*

Emotion Literate's Proclamation

 **I am vulnerable living in the unknown.**

Oh yes, I have my patterns, my familiars, my adaptive powers AND I am vulnerable living in the unknown. To hide, minimize, pretend that I am not vulnerable is to lie
to myself.
To lie, I must feed my fear and numb my sense-abilities, my ability to sense that I am vulnerable living in the unknown.
To not sense myself is to not be myself.
To not be myself is to ignore myself, forget myself, lose myself.
To lose myself is to lose my protection, my be-ing, and wear a mask.
To lose my protection, my being, and wear a mask I must be somebody else, somebody who is not vulnerable
not living in the unknown.
To be somebody who is
not vulnerable not living in the unknown,

I must act tougher, smarter,
more something or other.
To act tougher or smarter
I must believe that it is necessary to hurt
or defeat another in order to not be hurt
or defeated myself.
To let myself feel my vulnerability
is to remember my vulnerability
from long ago and how it was exploited,
bull-dozed over, not noticed.
I must remember or I will forget
that I am vulnerable living in the
unknown—still.
I must remember so that I can recognize myself.
To recognize myself is to
pay attention to myself.
To pay attention to myself is to
protect myself, to be with myself.
To protect myself, to be with myself,
I must know myself and what I need.
To know myself and what I need,
I must learn about myself.
To learn about myself, I must be open.
To be open, I must be vulnerable
living in the unknown.

Note: For further engagement with emotion literacy's foundational concepts in the *I Can* book, please explore Pamela Sackett's online curriculum called "My Alphabet to Freedom: Liberating the Language of Choice & Connection." A guided inquiry with original theatrical, musical and visual content as catalysts for self-reflective writing and discussion, the program focuses on twelve communication competencies which are synonymous with the twelve ways of this book.

Comments from online program participants:

...the steps provided to "stretch" one's mental door are great ways to think outside the box of being simply right or wrong...the lyrics in this section definitely do motivate me to encourage change in idle areas of my life... I swear this material could not be more applicable to my life...it's showing me how to look inward and be the observer...

...I have even more impetus to slow myself down in moments where learning and growth can be given air to breathe...I bring this awareness into my work conversations to foster clarity and alignment of understanding...

...the idea of "soft needs" is currently very important in my life...this does a great job of identifying what creates feelings and why they are so complex... love the audio clips...stimulating, fun, enlightening... like a Proust novel—a world, in parts, each of which I can enter and be at its center...

...I look forward to doing the exercises and reaping the rewards...

ELA's "My Alphabet to Freedom" curriculum is available by special arrangement. For more information:
info@emolit.org.

Partial list of beneficiaries of Pamela's musical, theatrical and literary works and presentations:

Alder Academy for At-Risk Youth

Antioch University

Banyen Books & Sound, Vancouver, B.C.

Big Brothers Big Sisters

Boys & Girls Clubs of Western Lane County

California Academy of Sciences San Francisco

Co-op Radio's World Poetry Cafe
    Vancouver, British Columbia

Elliot Bay Book Company

Film Archives:

—Academy of Motion Picture Arts & Sciences

—University of California, Los Angeles

International Human Learning Resources
    Network (Mexico)

King County Youth Detention Facility

KKNW 1150 AM, Teen Talk

Kutenai Art Therapy Institute, Nelson, Canada

National Association for Women in Psychology

North Rehabilitation Facility Seattle

Oregon Post Adoption Resource Center
Parent Enhancement Program (Oregon)
Permanente Journal Winter Vol 8 No.1 & 2
Powerful Schools
Salish Sea Ecosystem Film Festival (B.C.)
Seattle Children's Museum
Seattle Public Schools
Seattle Repertory Theatre Company
    Outreach & Education
Seattle University
Simon Fraser University (Canada)
Tacoma/Pierce County WA State
    Health Dept.
Theatre For Young Audiences Today
    (ASSITEJ/USA)
University of Washington
Washington Advocates for the Mentally Ill
Washington State Family Policy Council

Thank you for sharing your amazing work and helping us improve...the way you are not afraid to portray your emotion inspires me to do the same...I was impressed by the wide range of different formats you used for your pieces...I love your poems and songs... I really admired the beautiful language, concise dialogue, your many identities...I love how your work felt deeply personal and private, yet really relatable and attractive... made me instantly connect and pay attention...you and your characters' journeys gave me inspiration for my own and provided a powerful meditation on the self...

~University of Washington
Writing Program
(teen participants' comments to Pamela)

For information about or to request a presentation, workshop or consultation with Pamela for your group, company or organization, visit:
emolit.org/contact-us.html

Emotion Literacy Advocates (ELA) is a nonprofit 501(c)3 organization that began in Seattle via a small group of artists and activists at the turn of the millennium. ELA has expanded to include a pool of generative artists and social activists across the globe, working in concert with Pamela Sackett to create and produce learning tools that incorporate language art, music, theatre and visual arts and science. ELA's resources address cultural and environmental issues with self and social awareness for individuals, learning institutions, social-service agencies and broadcast media.

avatar art: Lisa Weyandt/Nrdy Byrd

CONNECT with EMOLIT.ORG

for more innovative arts-based
RESOURCES
free downloads
books
multi-media learning tools
including vignettes
& songbook movies
workshops + consultations
plus podcast episodes
featuring Pamela w/ hosts
in lively conversations

VISIT ELA's
YouTube channel & Instagram
@emotionliteracyadvocates

Image by Srishti Dokras
from
"Passageway Songbook Movie"
(virtual musical picture book)

www.ingramcontent.com/pod-product-compliance
Lightning Source LLC
Chambersburg PA
CBHW062104290426
44110CB00022B/2703